# JAPAN

## Travel Journal

## UNPLUG & WRITE

# WANDERLUST JOURNALS COLLECTION

WWW.WANDERLUST-JOURNALS.COM

WHEN WE TRAVEL
WE STOP BEING WHO WE ARE
TO BECOME BEING
WHO WE WANT TO BE.

AUG
7 PM

BY AIR MAIL

# INDEX

# IF FOUND
# PLEASE RETURN IT TO:

## Name:

------------------------------------------------------------

## Address:

------------------------------------------------------------

## Phone number:

------------------------------------------------------------

## Email address:

------------------------------------------------------------

# Trip Planner

# W?

# What? ( Do I want to learn from this trip)

---

---

## When? ( Do I travel?)

---

---

## Where? ( Do I go?)

---

---

## Why? ( Do I travel?)

---

---

# Checklist

## Things to do before leaving

# Family and Friends

## Telephone numbers

## ( in case I lose my phone )

# Packing list

## Things I'm taking with me

# CARRY-ON
## IMPORTANT DOCUMENTS AND NECESSITIES

# Hygiene and medicine

# Clothing

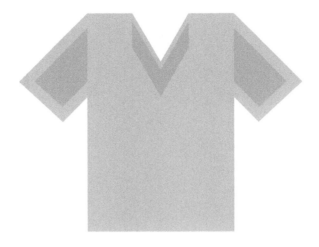

# MISCELLANEOUS

# Itinerary Overview

# MAPS

( Paste map)

# MY FAVOURITE LANDSCAPES

# My favourite museums

# RESTAURANTS I LOVE

# MY CHILLOUT PLACES

# SERENDIPITOUS TRAVEL MOMENTS:

Serendipity is an unexpected discovery when we are seeking something different.
The word emerged in 1700 from a Persian fairy tale, which takes place on an island called "Serendip", in which the protagonists solved all their problems through coincidences.

# WHAT IS MY SERENDIPITOUS MOMENT IN THIS TRIP?

# THINGS I DO WHILE TRAVELING BUT NOT AT HOME:

# Songs that inspire me on this trip:

# Cultural shock

## ( Things, People, habits I'm not used to see )

# Mood Tracker

# THINGS THAT MAKE ME HAPPY:

# THINGS THAT MAKE ME SAD:

# Things that make me angry:

# Things that make me Calm:

# COLOR ME WHEN
# STRESSED

## ( OR WAITING AT THE AIRPORT )

# DRAW WHATEVER IS MISSING

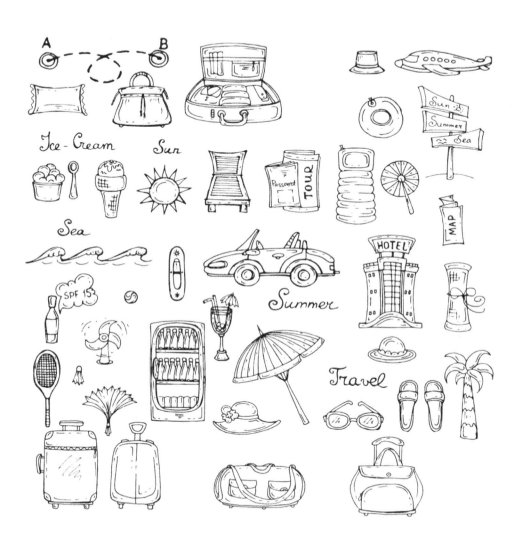

# DRAW WHATEVER IS MISSING

Ticket

Travel

Trip

Map

# My takeaway of this trip is:

# I HAVE LEARNED...

# FOR NEXT TRIP I WOULD AVOID...

# WHAT I LIKED THE MOST...

# COUNTRIES I HAVE VISITED IN MY LIFE...

( TO FILL IN )

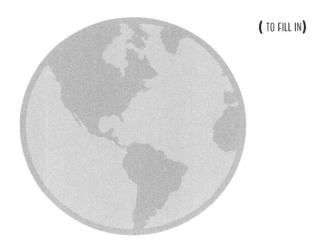

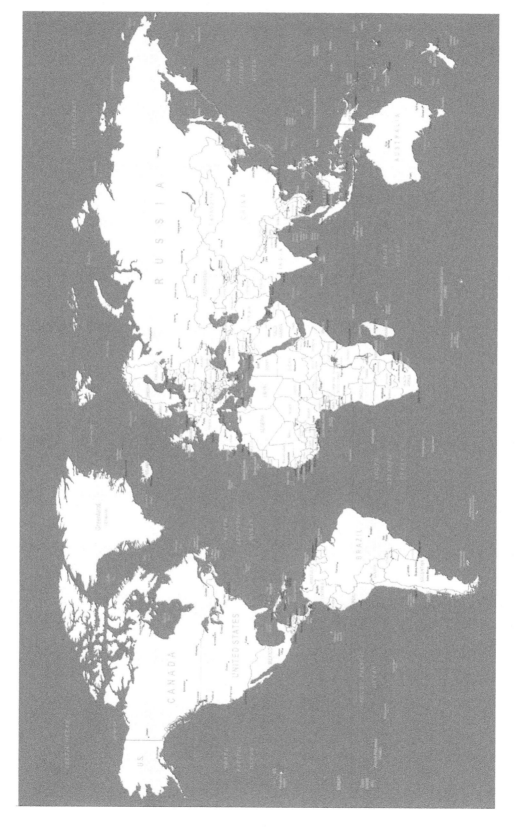

# MY BEST PHOTOS

# When?

# Where?

# WHEN?

# WHERE?

# WHEN?

# WHERE?

# WHEN?

# WHERE?

# WONDERFUL PEOPLE I MET ON THIS TRIP

NAME:

EMAIL:

COUNTRY:

HE / SHE MADE MY TRIP SPECIAL

BECAUSE...


NAME:

EMAIL:

COUNTRY:

HE / SHE MADE MY TRIP SPECIAL

BECAUSE...

NAME:

EMAIL:

COUNTRY:

HE / SHE MADE MY TRIP SPECIAL

BECAUSE...

NAME:

EMAIL:

COUNTRY:

HE / SHE MADE MY TRIP SPECIAL

BECAUSE...

# MY THOUGHTS

# My creative space

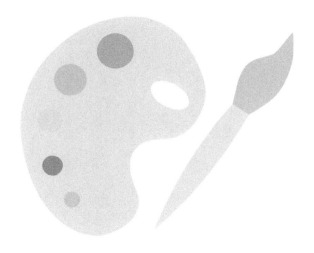

Thanks for leaving a review for this book
or sending us your feedback to:

contact@wanderlust-journals.com


Don´t forget to Check out

# The Wanderlust Journals collection

We have a journal for every moment of your life

# Get 30%off

## On your next Wanderlust Journal
## CODE: 4CTLX2K3

INSTRUCTIONS:

- Scan the QR CODE (or just enter Createspace store and search Wanderlust journals)
- In the checkout insert the code: 4CTLX2K3 and automatically save 30% in your purchase.

Made in the USA
Las Vegas, NV
04 June 2023

72968875R00069